GLYCEMIC INDEX CHART 2（

Scientific Verified Low GI Foods and Recipes For Diabetes Control, Weight Loss & Healthy Eating With A 28-Day Meal Plan

Alice McBride

Table of Contents

INTRODUCTION

The modern-day lifestyle is making it harder and harder for people to manage their weight and maintain healthy blood sugar levels.

According to the World Health Organization, over 650 million people around the world are living with diabetes, and over 1.2 billion people are living with prediabetes. With the alarming number of people suffering from weight-related issues and diabetes, it is essential to find a solution that can help people manage their health and weight. That's where Glycemic Index Foods fit in.

The Glycemic Index Food Guide Chart 2023 is a comprehensive guide to the glycemic index of different types of food. The glycemic index (GI) measures how quickly a food is broken down and absorbed into the bloodstream.

Foods that are high on the GI scale are broken down quickly, releasing their energy as glucose into the bloodstream, whereas foods that are low on the GI scale release their energy more slowly, providing a steady supply of energy.

This book provides an easy-to-understand explanation of the GI of different food types, allowing users to make informed decisions when it comes to their dietary choices.

This book is an invaluable resource for those looking to make informed dietary decisions and maintain a healthy lifestyle.

Also, "The Glycemic Index Food Guide Chart 2023" is the perfect solution for anyone who wants to manage their weight, blood sugar levels, and overall health. This Diet Book provides detailed information about *the glycemic index of various foods, and how to use that information to make healthy, nutritious food choices.* It also offers a 28-days eating plan, tips and recipes to help you achieve your health goals. With the help of this book, you can make informed decisions about what to eat and how to best take care of your body.

CHAPTER 1

Comprehensive Guide To The GI Diet And Its Benefits For Health And Wellness

Are you looking for a way to lose weight, maintain healthy blood sugar levels and have more energy? As someone who has struggled with all of the above, I have come to understand the importance of understanding the Glycemic Index (GI).

After experimenting with various diets and trying to find a solution to my health and wellness issues, I finally discovered the GI diet. This diet is based on the Glycemic Index – a system that ranks carbohydrates based on how quickly they affect your blood sugar levels. In this chapter, you'll learn how the GI diet works and how it can help you reach your health and wellness goals.

The GI diet is a highly effective way to control your blood sugar levels, lose weight, and increase your energy levels.

The Glycemic Index (GI) diet is a way of eating that focuses on foods with a low to moderate glycemic index.

GI is a measure of how quickly and how much a food can raise your blood sugar level. Foods with a high GI are broken down quickly and can cause a sharp rise in blood sugar levels, while foods with a low GI are broken down more slowly, allowing your blood sugar to remain more stable.

Low GI Foods

Low GI foods are those with a GI of 55 or less and include oats, lentils, beans, and most fruits and vegetables. Low GI foods are digested slowly, which leads to a gradual increase in blood sugar levels. Low GI foods are also high in fiber, which helps to keep you fuller for longer, and are generally thought to be healthier than high GI foods.

Medium GI Foods

Medium GI foods range from 56-69 on the GI scale and include whole wheat bread, brown rice, and some fruits and vegetables. Medium GI foods are digested at a moderate rate and can help to provide sustained energy throughout the day.

High GI Foods

High GI foods have a GI of 70 or more, and include white bread, white rice, and most processed and refined carbohydrates. High GI foods are digested quickly, which can lead to a rapid rise in blood sugar levels. While these foods can provide a quick energy boost, they can also cause a rapid drop in blood sugar levels after they are digested, which can leave you feeling tired and hungry.

When following a GI diet, it is important to focus on eating low to medium GI foods, as these are digested more slowly and can help to keep your blood sugar levels stable. Eating high GI foods should be limited to special occasions or as an occasional treat. Eating a balanced diet with a variety of foods is also important, as this will help to provide all of the essential nutrients your body needs.

What is the Glycemic Index?

The Glycemic Index (GI) is a numerical system of ranking foods based on how quickly and how much they raise a person's blood sugar level.

Foods are given a GI rating from 0 to 100, with a higher score meaning the food is more quickly digested and will cause a rapid rise in blood sugar.

Foods that are high on the GI scale are considered "fast-acting" carbohydrates, meaning they are digested quickly and cause a rapid rise in blood sugar. Examples of high GI foods include white bread, white rice, and sugary sodas and juices. Foods that are low on the GI scale are "slow-acting" carbohydrates, meaning they are digested more slowly and cause a more gradual rise in blood sugar. Examples of low GI foods include whole-grain breads, oats, legumes, and most fruits and vegetables.

The Glycemic Index is used by nutritionists, dietitians, and health care professionals to help people with diabetes and other conditions that require careful blood sugar control. By understanding the GI of different foods, people can better manage their blood sugar levels and choose foods that will provide slow, sustained energy rather than quick, short-lived spikes in blood sugar.

The GI of a food is affected by a variety of factors, including the degree of processing, the type of carbohydrate, the amount of fiber and fat in the food, and how ripe or mature the food is. For example, ripe fruit is typically higher on the GI scale than unripe fruit.

The Glycemic Index can be a useful tool for understanding how different foods affect your blood sugar, but it should not be used as a sole guide for food selection. Eating a variety of healthy, nutrient-dense foods is the best way to ensure good nutrition and optimal health.

The Benefits of a Low GI Diet

A low GI diet is a type of diet that focuses on foods with a low glycemic index (GI). Low GI foods are those that are slowly digested and absorbed, leading to a gradual rise in blood glucose levels. This type of diet has been linked to a number of health benefits, including weight loss, improved blood sugar control, and protection against heart disease and some forms of cancer.

1. Weight Loss: A low GI diet can help promote weight loss by making you feel full longer after eating. This is because low GI foods are digested more slowly, so they take longer to leave your stomach and enter the bloodstream. This means you don't get the same spike in blood sugar levels and subsequent crash that can lead to cravings and overeating.

2. Lower Blood Sugar Levels: A low GI diet can help improve blood sugar control in people with diabetes. This is because the slow digestion and absorption of low GI foods leads to a more gradual and sustained rise in blood sugar levels. This can help reduce the risk of dangerous blood sugar spikes and dips.

3. Reduced Risk of Heart Disease: A low GI diet may also reduce the risk of heart disease. Studies have shown that a low GI diet can lower cholesterol levels and reduce the risk of developing type 2 diabetes, both of which are risk factors for heart disease.

4. Cancer Protection: A low GI diet may also reduce the risk of certain types of cancer. Studies have shown that a low GI diet may help reduce the risk of breast cancer, colorectal cancer, and endometrial cancer.

Overall, a low GI diet can be a great way to improve your health and reduce your risk of certain diseases. The diet is based on eating foods that are slowly digested and absorbed, which can lead to a number of health benefits, including weight loss, improved blood sugar control, and protection against heart disease and some types of cancer.

How Foods Affect Your Blood Glucose Levels

As a person living with diabetes, you know how important it is to understand how foods affect your blood glucose levels. Eating the wrong types of food can lead to dangerously high or low blood sugar levels. It's essential to be aware of the foods that can cause your blood glucose levels to spike or drop.

For instance, carbohydrates are the primary source of energy for the body and can cause a rise in blood glucose levels. Examples of high-carbohydrate foods include bread, pasta, rice, sugary snacks, and fruits. Eating too much of these can cause your blood sugar to spike. It's important to watch your portions and consider making healthier carbohydrate choices, like whole grains and legumes.

On the flip side, protein has the opposite effect. Eating high-protein foods, such as lean meats, beans, and nuts, can cause a drop in blood glucose levels. This can be beneficial if you need to lower your blood sugar, but it can also be dangerous if you're already low.

To better manage your blood glucose levels, it's important to consider the types and amounts of foods you eat. You should also talk to your doctor or a nutritionist to develop a plan that works best for you.

Take the case of Mary, a 22-year lady living with diabetes. Mary was having trouble managing her blood sugar levels. After talking with her doctor and nutritionist, Mary was able to develop a meal plan that incorporated both carbohydrate and protein foods in the right amounts. Mary was able to successfully manage her blood glucose levels by following her meal plan.

By understanding how foods affect your blood glucose levels, you can take steps to make sure you're eating the right types and amounts of food. With the help of your healthcare team, you can successfully manage your blood glucose levels.

Foods That Are Low On The GI Scale

Foods that are low on the GI scale are those that cause a slower and steadier rise in blood sugar levels. Low GI foods, also referred to as 'slow carbs,' are broken down more slowly by the body, resulting in a slower and more gradual rise in blood sugar levels.

Eating low GI foods can help you to maintain stable blood sugar levels, which is beneficial for managing diabetes and increasing energy levels.

Low GI foods include:

• Whole grains such as oats, barley, and whole wheat bread.

• Legumes such as lentils, beans, and chickpeas.

• Fruits such as apples, oranges, and berries.

• Vegetables such as spinach, broccoli, and carrots.

• Nuts and seeds such as almonds and pumpkin seeds.

• Dairy products such as yogurt and cottage cheese.

• Lean proteins such as chicken, fish, and eggs.

• Healthy fats such as olive oil and avocados.

• Herbs and spices such as cinnamon, turmeric, and cumin.

Eating low GI foods can also help with weight loss. Low GI foods help to keep you feeling full for longer, reducing the temptation to snack between meals. They also help to regulate your blood sugar levels, which can reduce hunger and cravings.

Furthermore, low GI foods can also help you burn more fat for energy, as they release their energy more slowly than high GI foods.

CHAPTER 2

Tips for Making Low GI Meals

Low GI (glycemic index) meals are an important part of a healthy diet. They can help improve blood sugar control, reduce the risk of diabetes and heart disease, and provide sustained energy throughout the day. Making low GI meals is easy, but there are some tips to make sure you get the most out of your meals.

1. Choose complex carbohydrates. Complex carbohydrates, such as quinoa, buckwheat, and barley, are digested slower than simple carbohydrates, like white bread or white rice, and have a lower glycemic index. By replacing simple carbohydrates with complex carbohydrates, you can reduce the GI of your meal.

2. Choose whole grains. Whole grains, such as oats, brown rice, and whole wheat, are higher in fiber and vitamins than refined grains. Eating whole grains can help reduce the glycemic index of a meal, and can make you feel fuller for longer.

3. Include healthy fats. Adding healthy fats to a low GI meal can help to slow down digestion, which can help to reduce the glycemic index. Healthy fats include avocado, olive oil, nuts, and seeds.

4. Add protein. Protein helps to slow down digestion, which can help to reduce the glycemic index. Adding lean proteins like chicken, fish, and eggs to a low GI meal can help to keep you feeling full for longer.

5. Choose low GI fruits and vegetables. Fruits and vegetables are a great source of nutrients and can help to reduce the glycemic index of a meal. Low GI fruits and vegetables include apples, oranges, berries, carrots, peppers, and spinach.

6. Avoid processed foods. Processed foods are usually high in sugar and simple carbohydrates, which can raise the glycemic index of a meal. Aim to choose fresh and minimally processed foods, such as fruits, vegetables, whole grains, lean proteins, and healthy fats.

By following these tips, you can make low GI meals that are nutritious, delicious, and satisfying. Low GI meals can help to keep your blood sugar stable, reduce the risk of diabetes and heart disease, and provide sustained energy throughout the day.

Choosing the Right Macronutrients for the Low GI Diet

The low GI diet is a dietary approach that focuses on consuming foods with a low glycemic index. These foods are digested more slowly, causing a gradual release of glucose into the bloodstream which helps to maintain steady energy levels and avoid spikes in blood sugar. It is important to select the right macronutrients when following a low GI diet in order to ensure that you are getting the nutrients your body needs while avoiding foods with a high glycemic index.

The best macronutrients for a low GI diet are those that are *high in fiber, low in sugar, and contain complex carbohydrates such as whole grains, legumes, and vegetables.* These foods provide slow-release energy and help keep blood sugar levels steady. When selecting your macronutrients, it is important to focus on nutrient-dense foods that are rich in vitamins and minerals.

High-fiber carbohydrates such as oats, quinoa, barley, and whole wheat pasta, are all great choices for a low GI diet.

These carbohydrates are digested more slowly and can help to stabilize blood sugar levels. Legumes such as beans, lentils, and chickpeas are also a good source of fiber and are rich in protein, making them an ideal macronutrient for the low GI diet.

Healthy fats such as olive oil, avocado, nuts, and seeds are also important macronutrients for the low GI diet. These fats help to slow the absorption of glucose and provide essential fatty acids that the body needs. Healthy proteins such as lean meats, fish, and eggs are also important macronutrients and can help to keep you feeling full and energized.

Including a variety of macronutrients in your diet is essential for good health and the low GI diet. Eating the right combination of carbohydrates, fats, and proteins can help to maintain steady energy levels and keep your blood sugar levels stable.

Choosing The Right Micronutrients for the Low GI Diet

Choosing the right micronutrients in a low glycemic diet is essential for optimal health and weight loss. Micronutrients are vitamins and minerals that are essential for the body to function properly. They are found in many foods, but some are more beneficial than others.

A low glycemic diet is one that is low in carbohydrates and high in healthy fats and proteins. This type of diet can help to reduce blood sugar levels, reduce inflammation, and improve overall health.

When choosing the right micronutrients for a low glycemic diet, it is important to focus on foods that are high in vitamins and minerals, such as fruits and vegetables.

Fruits and vegetables are packed with vitamins, minerals, and antioxidants that help to fight disease and promote health. Whole grains, legumes, nuts, and seeds are also excellent sources of micronutrients.

Additionally, foods such as fish, eggs, and low-fat dairy products are good sources of protein and healthy fats.

In addition to selecting foods that are rich in micronutrients, it is important to pay attention to the glycemic index of foods. The glycemic index is a measure of how quickly a food will raise your blood sugar level. Foods with a low glycemic index, such as whole grains, legumes, and fruits, are better choices than those with a high glycemic index, such as white bread and sweets.

To ensure that you are getting the right micronutrients in a low glycemic diet, it is important to eat a variety of foods. Eating a variety of fruits, vegetables, whole grains, legumes, nuts, and seeds will provide you with the essential vitamins and minerals that your body needs.

List of Micronutrients for a Low Glycemic Diet:

1. Fruits and vegetables
2. Whole grains
3. Legumes
4. Nuts and seeds
5. Fish
6. Eggs
7. Low-fat dairy products
8. Healthy fats (olive oil, avocado, nuts)
9. Herbs and spices (garlic, turmeric, ginger)
10. Dark chocolate
11. Tea and coffee
12. Fermented foods (yogurt, kefir, sauerkraut)

FAQS

What Does it Mean to Have a High or Low Glycemic Index?

Answer: Foods with a high GI will cause a rapid rise in blood sugar levels, while foods with a low GI will cause a slower, steadier rise.

How can I incorporate low GI foods into my diet?

Answer: Start by eating more fruits and vegetables with every meal. Replace white bread and pasta with whole grain options. Choose legumes and dairy products instead of high-sugar snacks.

Can I still eat high GI foods?

Answer: Yes, you can still eat high GI foods. However, you should be mindful of portion sizes, as these foods can cause a spike in blood sugar levels.

Are all carbohydrates considered low GI?

Answer: No, not all carbohydrates have a low GI. Some carbohydrates, such as white potatoes, have a high GI.

Are there any foods that are both low GI and high in protein?

Answer: Yes, there are several foods that are both low GI and high in protein, such as legumes, dairy products, nuts, and seeds.

What Types of Foods Should I Avoid to Have a Low-Glycemic Diet?

Answer: You should avoid processed foods, sugary snacks and beverages, white bread and pasta, and white potatoes to have a low-glycemic diet.

What are Some Healthy Low-Glycemic Snack Ideas?

Answer: Some healthy low-glycemic snack ideas include nuts, seeds, plain yogurt, hard-boiled eggs, fruits and vegetables, hummus, and whole grain crackers.

Are There Any Low-Glycemic Alternatives to Processed Foods?

Answer: Yes, there are many low-glycemic alternatives to processed foods, such as whole grains, legumes, fruits and vegetables, and dairy products.

CHAPTER 3

SCIENTIFIC VERIFIED FOODS TO INCLUDE IN YOUR LOW GLYCEMIC DIET

Eating Low Glycemic and Anti-Inflammatory Foods

The GI (Glycemic Index) diet is a way of eating that focuses on choosing foods that are low on the glycemic index and anti-inflammatory.

These foods are thought to help keep blood sugar levels steady, reduce inflammation, and reduce the risk of diabetes, heart disease, and other health problems. The diet includes eating plenty of fruits and vegetables, whole grains, lean proteins, and healthy fats.

Eating low-glycemic and anti-inflammatory foods can help provide the body with the nutrients it needs, while also avoiding the spikes in blood sugar and inflammation that can be caused by some high-glycemic foods.

Avoiding High Glycemic and Inflammatory Foods

Avoiding high glycemic and inflammatory foods is an important part of the GI diet. High glycemic foods are those that cause a rapid spike in blood sugar and can lead to weight gain and other health problems.

Inflammatory foods can trigger an increase in inflammation, which can lead to chronic health conditions. The GI diet recommends avoiding processed carbohydrates and sugars, including white bread, pasta, and processed snacks.

Other high glycemic and inflammatory foods to avoid include fried and processed meats, refined oils, and foods high in saturated fat. Eating a diet that is rich in vegetables, fruits, lean proteins, and healthy fats is an important part of the GI diet and can help promote good health.

Eating Whole and Minimally Processed Foods

The GI diet recommends eating minimally processed and whole foods to improve overall health. Eating whole foods means selecting foods in their natural state, or as close to their natural state as possible.

This includes fruits, vegetables, whole grains, legumes, nuts and seeds, and lean proteins. Minimally processed foods are those that have been processed as little as possible, such as 100% whole wheat bread, low-fat yogurt, and frozen vegetables without added sauces.

This type of diet helps to reduce the amount of refined sugars, unhealthy fats, and artificial ingredients in the diet, which can help improve overall health.

Your Low Glycemic Index Shopping List

1 - Meat, Poultry and Seafood

1. Skinless Chicken (GI: 0)

2. Boneless Fish (GI: 0)

3. Lean Ground Beef (GI: 0)

4. Pork Tenderloin (GI: 0)

5. Turkey Breast (GI: 0)

6. Tilapia (GI: 0)

7. Lobster (GI: 0)

8. Salmon (GI: 0)

9. Shrimp (GI: 0)

10. Venison (GI: 0)

2 - Vegetables and Vegetable Products

1. Broccoli (GI: 15)
2. Carrots (GI: 16)
3. Spinach (GI: 15)
4. Romaine Lettuce (GI: 15)
5. Eggplant (GI: 15)
6. Zucchini (GI: 15)
7. Celery (GI: 15)
8. Cauliflower (GI: 15)
9. Green Beans (GI: 15)
10. Red Bell Peppers (GI: 10)

3 - Fruit and Fruit Products

1. Apples (GI: 38)

2. Pears (GI: 38)

3. Oranges (GI: 40)

4. Strawberries (GI: 40)

5. Blueberries (GI: 40)

6. Raspberries (GI: 40)

7. Peaches (GI: 42)

8. Plums (GI: 40)

9. Cherries (GI: 22)

10. Kiwi (GI: 42)

4 - Drinks & Beverages

1. Water (GI: 0)

2. Green Tea (GI: 0)

3. Unsweetened Almond Milk (GI: 0)

4. Unsweetened Coconut Milk (GI: 0)

5. Unsweetened Cashew Milk (GI: 0)

6. Unsweetened Hemp Milk (GI: 0)

7. Unsweetened Soy Milk (GI: 0)

8. Unsweetened Rice Milk (GI: 0)

9. Unsweetened Oat Milk (GI: 0)

10. Unsweetened Flax Milk (GI: 0)

5 - Dairy Products

1. Plain Greek Yogurt (GI: 0)

2. Skim Milk (GI: 32)

3. Cottage Cheese (GI: 15)

4. Low-Fat Cheese (GI: 0)

5. Ricotta Cheese (GI: 0)

6. Feta Cheese (GI: 0)

7. Goat Cheese (GI: 0)

8. Mozzarella Cheese (GI: 0)

9. Cream Cheese (GI: 0)

10. Parmesan Cheese (GI: 0)

6 - Cereals, Rice & Grains

1. Quinoa (GI: 53)

2. Basmati Rice (GI: 58)

3. Steel Cut Oats (GI: 55)

4. Rolled Oats (GI: 55)

5. Wild Rice (GI: 54)

6. Brown Rice (GI: 50)

7. Barley (GI: 25)

8. Spelt (GI: 35)

9. Buckwheat (GI: 50)

10. Millet (GI: 71)

7 - Bread

1. Rye Bread (GI: 40)

2. Whole Wheat Bread (GI: 69)

3. Multigrain Bread (GI: 51)

4. Sourdough Bread (GI: 41)

5. Pumpernickel Bread (GI: 53)

6. Oat Bran Bread (GI: 50)

7. Flaxseed Bread (GI: 47)

8. Sprouted Grain Bread (GI: 45)

9. Buckwheat Bread (GI: 45)

10. Gluten-Free Bread (GI: 62)

8 - Breakfast Cereals

1. All-Bran (GI: 37)

2. Oat Bran (GI: 55)

3. Wheat Bran (GI: 40)

4. Shredded Wheat (GI: 65)

5. Wheat Germ (GI: 42)

6. Muesli (GI: 42)

7. Puffed Rice (GI: 79)

8. Puffed Wheat (GI: 75)

9. Oatmeal (GI: 55)

10. Corn Flakes (GI: 81)

9 - Mixed Meals & Convenience Food

1. Frozen Meals (GI: Varies)

2. Microwave Dinners (GI: Varies)

3. Soup (GI: Varies)

4. Pizza (GI: Varies)

5. Burrito (GI: Varies)

6. Salad (GI: Varies)

7. Sandwich (GI: Varies)

8. Wraps (GI: Varies)

9. Sushi (GI: Varies)

10. Noodle Bowls (GI: Varies)

10 - Legumes

1. Lentils (GI: 32)

2. Kidney Beans (GI: 29)

3. Chickpeas (GI: 33)

4. Black Beans (GI: 30)

5. Pinto Beans (GI: 46)

6. Navy Beans (GI: 39)

7. Black-Eyed Peas (GI: 33)

8. Split Peas (GI: 32)

9. Lima Beans (GI: 32)

10. Fava Beans (GI: 30)

11 - Canned Food

1. Canned Vegetables (GI: Varies)
2. Canned Beans (GI: Varies)
3. Canned Fruit (GI: Varies)
4. Canned Soup (GI: Varies)
5. Canned Fish (GI: Varies)
6. Canned Tuna (GI: 0)
7. Canned Salmon (GI: 0)
8. Canned Crab (GI: 0)
9. Canned Shrimp (GI: 0)
10. Canned Clams (GI: 0)

12 - Fresh Herbs

1. Oregano (GI: 0)

2. Parsley (GI: 0)

3. Basil (GI: 0)

4. Dill (GI: 0)

5. Rosemary (GI: 0)

6. Thyme (GI: 0)

7. Sage (GI: 0)

8. Mint (GI: 0)

9. Tarragon (GI: 0)

10. Coriander (GI: 0)

13 - Condiments, oils, fats

1. Extra Virgin Olive Oil (GI: 0)
2. Coconut Oil (GI: 0)
3. Avocado Oil (GI: 0)
4. Walnut Oil (GI: 0)
5. Almond Oil (GI: 0)
6. Mustard (GI: 0)
7. Apple Cider Vinegar (GI: 0)
8. Balsamic Vinegar (GI: 0)
9. Hummus (GI: 0)
10. Tahini (GI: 0)

CHAPTER 4

The Low GI Recipes for Diabetes Control, Weight Loss, and Healthy Eating

Recipes contained in this cookbook focus on providing healthy, nutritious recipes with a low glycemic index (GI).

This cookbook takes into account the special dietary needs of people with diabetes, weight loss and inflammation, while still providing delicious, satisfying meals. It includes over 60 recipes, which are designed to be healthful and easy to prepare with ingredients that can be found in most grocery stores.

Each recipe is labeled with its GI value, so readers can choose the recipes that are best suited to their health needs.

Breakfast Recipes

1. Overnight Oats

Serves: 2 | Prep Time: 5 minutes

Ingredients (GI value):

- 1/2 cup rolled oats (48)
- 1 cup almond milk (35)
- 1/2 teaspoon ground cinnamon (0)
- 1 tablespoon honey (55)
- 1/4 cup chopped almonds (15)
- 1/2 teaspoon vanilla extract (0)

Directions:

1. Place the oats, almond milk, cinnamon, honey and vanilla extract in a bowl and stir to combine.

2. Cover the bowl and place it in the refrigerator overnight.

3. When ready to eat, divide the oats between two bowls and top with the chopped almonds.

2. Avocado Toast

Serves: 2 | Prep Time: 5 minutes

Ingredients (GI value):

•2 slices whole grain bread (53)

•1 ripe avocado (3)

•1 tablespoon olive oil (15)

•1/4 teaspoon sea salt (0)

•1/4 teaspoon freshly ground black pepper (0)

Directions:

1. Toast the bread until golden brown.

2. Meanwhile, mash the avocado in a small bowl.

3. Spread the mashed avocado on the toast and drizzle with olive oil.

4. Sprinkle with salt and pepper.

3. Egg Muffins

Serves: 4 | Prep Time: 10 minutes | Cook Time: 15 minutes

Ingredients (GI value):

- 6 large eggs (0)
- 1/2 cup chopped bell pepper (0)
- 1/2 cup chopped onion (0)
- 1/2 cup shredded cheese (0)
- 1/4 teaspoon sea salt (0)
- 1/4 teaspoon freshly ground black pepper (0)
- 2 tablespoons olive oil (15)

Directions:

1. Preheat oven to 350 degrees F.

2. Grease a muffin pan with olive oil.

3. In a large bowl, whisk together eggs, bell pepper, onion, cheese, salt, and pepper.

4. Divide the mixture evenly among the muffin cups.

5. Bake for 15 minutes, or until the eggs are set.

4. Peanut Butter and Banana Toast

Serves: 1 | Prep Time: 5 minutes

Ingredients (GI value):

- 1 slice whole grain bread (53)

- 1 tablespoon peanut butter (7)
- 1/2 banana, sliced (42)
- 1 tablespoon honey (55)

Directions:

1. Toast the bread until golden brown.

2. Spread the peanut butter on the toast and top with the banana slices.

3. Drizzle with honey.

5. Cottage Cheese with Berries

Serves: 1 | Prep Time: 5 minutes

Ingredients (GI value):

- 1/2 cup low fat cottage cheese (13)
- 1/2 cup fresh blueberries (53)
- 1/4 cup chopped almonds (15)
- 1 tablespoon honey (55)

Directions:

1. Place the cottage cheese in a bowl and top with blueberries, almonds, and honey.

2. Stir to combine and enjoy.

6. Omelet with Vegetables

Serves: 1 | Prep Time: 5 minutes | Cook Time: 10 minutes

Ingredients (GI value):

•2 large eggs (0)

•1/2 cup chopped bell pepper (0)

•1/4 cup chopped onion (0)

•1/4 cup shredded cheese (0)

•1 tablespoon olive oil (15)

•1/4 teaspoon sea salt (0)

•1/4 teaspoon freshly ground black pepper (0)

Directions:

1. Heat the olive oil in a small skillet over medium heat.

2. Add the bell pepper and onion and cook until softened, about 3 minutes.

3. Meanwhile, whisk together the eggs, cheese, salt, and pepper in a small bowl.

4. Pour the egg mixture into the skillet and cook until the eggs are set, about 5 minutes.

5. Flip the omelet and cook for an additional 2 minutes.

7. Greek Yogurt with Nuts and Seeds

Serves: 1 | Prep Time: 5 minutes

Ingredients (GI value):

• 1 cup Greek yogurt (14)

• 2 tablespoons chopped walnuts (15)

• 2 tablespoons sunflower seeds (15)

• 1 tablespoon honey (55)

Directions:

1. Place the Greek yogurt in a bowl and top with walnuts, sunflower seeds, and honey.

2. Stir to combine and enjoy.

8. Steel-Cut Oatmeal with Fruit

Serves: 1 | Prep Time: 5 minutes | Cook Time: 10 minutes

Ingredients (GI value):

• 1/4 cup steel-cut oats (49)

• 1 cup water (0)

• 1/4 teaspoon ground cinnamon (0)

• 1/4 cup diced apple (38)

• 1/4 cup diced pear (38)

•1 tablespoon honey (55)

Directions:

1. Place the oats, water, and cinnamon in a small saucepan and bring to a boil.

2. Reduce heat to low and simmer for 10 minutes, stirring occasionally.

3. Remove from heat and stir in the diced apples and pears.

4. Drizzle with honey and enjoy.

9. Kale and Sweet Potato Frittata

Serves: 4 | Prep Time: 10 minutes | Cook Time: 25 minutes

Ingredients (GI value):

•4 large eggs (0)

•1/4 cup chopped kale (0)

•1/4 cup diced sweet potato (44)

•1/4 cup shredded cheese (0)

•1 tablespoon olive oil (15)

•1/4 teaspoon sea salt (0)

•1/4 teaspoon freshly ground black pepper (0)

Directions:

1. Preheat oven to 350 degrees F.

2. Heat the olive oil in a medium skillet over medium heat.

3. Add the kale and sweet potato and cook until softened, about 7 minutes.

4. Meanwhile, whisk together the eggs, cheese, salt, and pepper in a small bowl.

5. Pour the egg mixture into the skillet and cook until the eggs are set, about 5 minutes.

6. Transfer the skillet to the oven and bake for 15 minutes, or until the eggs are cooked through.

10. Whole-Grain Pancakes with Berries

Serves: 4 | Prep Time: 10 minutes | Cook Time: 10 minutes

Ingredients (GI value):

- 1 cup whole wheat flour (48)
- 1 teaspoon baking powder (0)
- 1/2 teaspoon baking soda (0)
- 1/4 teaspoon sea salt (0)
- 1 cup almond milk (35)
- 1 tablespoon honey (55)
- 1/2 teaspoon vanilla extract (0)
- 1/2 cup fresh blueberries (53)

•1 tablespoon butter (0)

Directions:

1. In a medium bowl, whisk together the flour, baking powder, baking soda, and salt.
2. In a small bowl, whisk together the almond milk, honey, and vanilla extract.
3. Add the wet ingredients to the dry ingredients and stir until just combined.
4. Heat the butter in a large skillet over medium heat.
5. Drop the batter by 1/4 cupfuls into the skillet and top with the blueberries.
6. Cook for 2-3 minutes, or until the edges are golden brown.
7. Flip the pancakes and cook for an additional 2 minutes, or until golden brown.

Lunch Recipes

1. Chicken and Roasted Vegetables

Serves: 4 | Prep Time: 10 minutes | Cook Time: 25 minutes

Ingredients (GI Value):

- 4-6 chicken thighs (GI: 0)

- 2 bell peppers, sliced (GI: 15)

- 2 zucchini, sliced (GI: 15)

- 2 onions, sliced (GI: 15)

- 2 tablespoons olive oil (GI: 0)

- 1 teaspoon garlic powder (GI: 0)

- 1 teaspoon oregano (GI: 0)

• Salt and pepper to taste

Directions:

1. Preheat oven to 400°F (200°C).

2. Place chicken thighs on a baking sheet.

3. In a separate bowl, mix together bell peppers, zucchini, onions, olive oil, garlic powder, oregano, salt, and pepper.

4. Place vegetables around chicken on baking sheet.

5. Bake for 25 minutes or until chicken is cooked through and vegetables are roasted.

2. Tuna Salad

Serves: 4 | Prep Time: 10 minutes

Ingredients (GI Value):

• 2 cans tuna, drained (GI: 0)

• 1/4 cup red onion, diced (GI: 15)

• 2 tablespoons olive oil (GI: 0)

• 2 tablespoons lemon juice (GI: 0)

• 2 tablespoons capers (GI: 0)

• 1 tablespoon dijon mustard (GI: 0)

• Salt and pepper to taste

Directions:

1. In a bowl, mix together tuna, red onion, olive oil, lemon juice, capers, dijon mustard, salt, and pepper.

2. Serve on top of a bed of lettuce or in a sandwich.

3. Egg Salad

Serves: 4 | Prep Time: 10 minutes

Ingredients (GI Value):

• 8 hard-boiled eggs, peeled and chopped (GI: 0)

• 1/4 cup celery, diced (GI: 10)

• 2 tablespoons olive oil (GI: 0)

• 2 tablespoons dijon mustard (GI: 0)

• 2 tablespoons lemon juice (GI: 0)

• Salt and pepper to taste

Directions:

1. In a bowl, mix together eggs, celery, olive oil, dijon mustard, lemon juice, salt, and pepper.

2. Serve on top of a bed of lettuce or in a sandwich.

4. Avocado Toast

Serves: 1 | Prep Time: 5 minutes

Ingredients (GI Value):

• 1 slice whole wheat bread (GI: 71)

• 1/2 avocado (GI: 0)

• 2 tablespoons olive oil (GI: 0)

• 1 tablespoon lemon juice (GI: 0)

• Salt and pepper to taste

Directions:

1. Toast the bread in a toaster.

2. Slice avocado in half and remove the pit.

3. Mash the avocado in a bowl.

4. Add olive oil, lemon juice, salt, and pepper and mix together.

5. Spread the avocado mixture on top of the toast.

5. Greek Salad

Serves: 4 | Prep Time: 10 minutes

Ingredients (GI Value):

- 1 cucumber, chopped (GI: 15)
- 1 cup cherry tomatoes, halved (GI: 15)
- 1/2 red onion, diced (GI: 15)
- 1/2 cup kalamata olives (GI: 0)
- 1/4 cup feta cheese (GI: 0)
- 2 tablespoons olive oil (GI: 0)
- 2 tablespoons lemon juice (GI: 0)
- 1 teaspoon dried oregano (GI: 0)
- Salt and pepper to taste

Directions:

1. In a bowl, mix together cucumber, tomatoes, red onion, olives, feta cheese, olive oil, lemon juice, oregano, salt, and pepper.

2. Serve on top of a bed of lettuce or with crusty bread.

6. Salmon with Roasted Sweet Potatoes

Serves: 4 | Prep Time: 10 minutes | Cook Time: 30 minutes

Ingredients (GI Value):

- 4 salmon fillets (GI: 0)

- 2 sweet potatoes, diced (GI: 53)

- 2 tablespoons olive oil (GI: 0)

- 2 teaspoons garlic powder (GI: 0)

- 2 teaspoons oregano (GI: 0)

- Salt and pepper to taste

Directions:

1. Preheat oven to 400°F (200°C).

2. Place salmon fillets on a baking sheet.

3. In a separate bowl, mix together sweet potatoes, olive oil, garlic powder, oregano, salt, and pepper.

4. Place sweet potatoes around salmon on baking sheet.

5. Bake for 30 minutes or until salmon is cooked through and sweet potatoes are roasted.

7. Cauliflower Rice Bowl

Serves: 4 | Prep Time: 10 minutes | Cook Time: 15 minutes

Ingredients (GI Value):

- 2 cups cauliflower, grated (GI: 15)

- 2 tablespoons olive oil (GI: 0)

- 1 teaspoon garlic powder (GI: 0)

- 1 teaspoon oregano (GI: 0)

- Salt and pepper to taste

- 1/2 cup cooked black beans (GI: 0)

- 1/4 cup diced red onion (GI: 15)

- 1/4 cup diced tomatoes (GI: 15)

- 1/4 cup feta cheese (GI: 0)

Directions:

1. Preheat oven to 400°F (200°C).

2. Place grated cauliflower on a baking sheet.

3. In a separate bowl, mix together olive oil, garlic powder, oregano, salt, and pepper.

4. Pour mixture over cauliflower and mix together.

5. Bake for 15 minutes or until cauliflower is cooked through.

6. In a bowl, mix together black beans, red onion, tomatoes, and feta cheese.

7. Serve cauliflower rice topped with bean mixture.

8. Cucumber and Tomato Salad

Serves: 4 | Prep Time: 10 minutes

Ingredients (GI Value):

- 2 cucumbers, diced (GI: 15)

- 2 cups cherry tomatoes, halved (GI: 15)

- 2 tablespoons olive oil (GI: 0)

- 1 tablespoon lemon juice (GI: 0)

- 1 teaspoon dried oregano (GI: 0)

- Salt and pepper to taste

Directions:

1. In a bowl, mix together cucumbers, tomatoes, olive oil, lemon juice, oregano, salt, and pepper.

2. Serve on top of a bed of lettuce or with crusty bread.

9. Lentil Soup

Serves: 4 | Prep Time: 10 minutes | Cook Time: 45 minutes

Ingredients (GI Value):

- 2 tablespoons olive oil (GI: 0)

- 1 onion, diced (GI: 15)

- 2 cloves garlic, minced (GI: 0)

- 2 carrots, diced (GI: 15)

- 2 stalks celery, diced (GI: 10)

- 1 teaspoon dried oregano (GI: 0)

- 1 teaspoon dried thyme (GI: 0)

- 1 cup dried lentils (GI: 0)

- 4 cups vegetable broth (GI: 0)

- Salt and pepper to taste

Directions:

1. Heat olive oil in a large saucepan over medium heat.

2. Add onion and garlic and cook until softened.

3. Add carrots, celery, oregano, and thyme and cook for another 5 minutes.

4. Add lentils and vegetable broth and bring to a boil.

5. Reduce heat to low and simmer for 45 minutes or until lentils are cooked through.

6. Season with salt and pepper to taste.

10. Quinoa Burrito Bowl

Serves: 4 | Prep Time: 10 minutes | Cook Time: 20 minutes

Ingredients (GI Value):

- 2 cups quinoa (GI: 53)

- 4 cups vegetable broth (GI: 0)

- 2 tablespoons olive oil (GI: 0)

- 1 onion, diced (GI: 15)

- 2 cloves garlic, minced (GI: 0)

- 2 bell peppers, chopped (GI: 15)

- 2 cups cherry tomatoes, halved (GI: 15)

- 1/2 cup cooked black beans (GI: 0)

- 1/4 cup feta cheese (GI: 0)

- 2 tablespoons lemon juice (GI: 0)

- 1 teaspoon dried oregano (GI: 0)

- Salt and pepper to taste

Directions:

1. In a saucepan, bring quinoa and vegetable broth to a boil.

2. Reduce heat to low and cover. Simmer for 20 minutes or until quinoa is cooked through.

3. Heat olive oil in a large skillet over medium heat.

4. Add onion and garlic and cook until softened.

5. Add bell peppers, tomatoes, black beans, feta cheese, lemon juice, oregano, salt, and pepper and cook for another 5 minutes.

6. Serve quinoa topped with vegetable mixture.

Dinner Recipes

1. Mediterranean Baked Salmon with Avocado and Tomatoes

Serves: 4 | Prep time: 15 minutes | Cook time: 15 minutes

Ingredients with GI value:

- Salmon fillets (GI: 0)
- Tomatoes (GI: 15)
- Avocado (GI: 0-15)
- Olive oil (GI: 0)
- Garlic (GI: 0)
- Salt and pepper (GI: 0)
- Thyme (GI: 0)

Directions:

1. Preheat oven to 400°F.

2. Place salmon fillets on a baking sheet lined with parchment paper.

3. Drizzle with olive oil and sprinkle with salt, pepper, and thyme.

4. Slice tomatoes and avocado and arrange around the salmon.

5. Bake for 15 minutes or until the salmon is cooked through.

6. Serve with garlic bread or a side salad.

2. Quinoa Stuffed Peppers

Serves: 4 | Prep time: 15 minutes | Cook time: 25 minutes

Ingredients with GI value:

- Bell peppers (GI: 0)

- Quinoa (GI: 53)

- Olive oil (GI: 0)

- Onion (GI: 10)

- Garlic (GI: 0)

- Tomatoes (GI: 15)

- Salt and pepper (GI: 0)

• Cheese (GI: 0)

Directions:

1. Preheat oven to 375°F.

2. Cut the tops off of the peppers and remove the seeds.

3. Cook the quinoa according to package instructions.

4. Heat olive oil in a skillet over medium heat.

5. Add the onion and garlic and cook until soft.

6. Add the tomatoes, salt, and pepper and cook for an additional 5 minutes.

7. Add the cooked quinoa and stir until combined.

8. Fill the peppers with the quinoa mixture and place in a baking dish.

9. Top with cheese and bake for 25 minutes.

10. Serve warm.

3. Roasted Vegetable and Feta Cheese Salad

Serves: 4 | Prep time: 15 minutes | Cook time: 25 minutes

Ingredients with GI value:

• Carrots (GI: 16)

• Sweet potatoes (GI: 44)

- Broccoli (GI: 15)

- Olive oil (GI: 0)

- Feta cheese (GI: 0)

- Lemon juice (GI: 0)

- Salt and pepper (GI: 0)

Directions:

1. Preheat oven to 425°F.

2. Cut the carrots, sweet potatoes, and broccoli into small cubes.

3. Place on a baking sheet lined with parchment paper and drizzle with olive oil.

4. Roast in the oven for 25 minutes or until the vegetables are tender.

5. Transfer to a bowl and add the feta cheese and lemon juice.

6. Toss to combine and season with salt and pepper.

7. Serve warm or at room temperature.

4. Creamy Butternut Squash Soup

Serves: 4 | Prep time: 15 minutes | Cook time: 25 minutes

Ingredients with GI value:

• Butternut squash (GI: 53)

• Olive oil (GI: 0)

• Onion (GI: 10)

• Garlic (GI: 0)

• Vegetable broth (GI: 0)

• Coconut milk (GI: 0)

• Salt and pepper (GI: 0)

Directions:

1. Preheat oven to 375°F.

2. Cut the butternut squash into cubes and place on a baking sheet.

3. Drizzle with olive oil and sprinkle with salt and pepper.

4. Roast in the oven for 25 minutes or until the squash is tender.

5. Heat olive oil in a pot over medium heat.

6. Add the onion and garlic and cook until softened.

7. Add the roasted squash and vegetable broth and bring to a simmer.

8. Reduce the heat to low and add the coconut milk.

9. Stir until combined and simmer for 10 minutes.

10. Puree the soup with an immersion blender until creamy.

11. Serve warm.

5. Cauliflower Fried Rice

Serves: 4 | Prep time: 15 minutes | Cook time: 15 minutes

Ingredients with GI value:

• Cauliflower (GI: 0)

• Olive oil (GI: 0)

• Onion (GI: 10)

• Garlic (GI: 0)

• Carrots (GI: 16)

• Peas (GI: 0)

• Soy sauce (GI: 0)

• Salt and pepper (GI: 0)

Directions:

1. Place the cauliflower in a food processor and pulse until it resembles rice.

2. Heat olive oil in a large skillet over medium heat.

3. Add the onion and garlic and cook until softened.

4. Add the carrots and peas and cook for an additional 5 minutes.

5. Add the cauliflower "rice" and cook for 5 minutes.

6. Add the soy sauce, salt, and pepper.

7. Stir until combined and cook for an additional 5 minutes.

8. Serve warm.

6. Veggie Burgers

Serves: 4 | Prep time: 15 minutes | Cook time: 10 minutes

Ingredients with GI value:

• Black beans (GI: 0)

• Quinoa (GI: 53)

• Onion (GI: 10)

• Garlic (GI: 0)

• Carrots (GI: 16)

• Cilantro (GI: 0)

• Salt and pepper (GI: 0)

• Olive oil (GI: 0)

Directions:

1. Place the black beans in a food processor and pulse until they are mashed.

2. Cook the quinoa according to package instructions.

3. Heat olive oil in a skillet over medium heat.

4. Add the onion, garlic, and carrots and cook until softened.

5. In a large bowl, combine the mashed beans, cooked quinoa, cooked vegetables, cilantro, salt, and pepper.

6. Form the mixture into patties.

7. Heat a large skillet over medium heat and cook the patties until golden brown, flipping once.

8. Serve on a bun with your favorite toppings.

7. Zucchini Noodles with Pesto

Serves: 4 | Prep time: 15 minutes | Cook time: 5 minutes

Ingredients with GI value:

- Zucchini (GI: 0)

- Basil pesto (GI: 0)

- Olive oil (GI: 0)

- Garlic (GI: 0)

- Parmesan cheese (GI: 0)

- Salt and pepper (GI: 0)

Directions:

1. Use a spiralizer or vegetable peeler to make zucchini noodles.

2. In a large bowl, combine the pesto, olive oil, garlic, parmesan cheese, salt, and pepper.

3. Add the zucchini noodles and stir until evenly coated.

4. Heat a large skillet over medium heat.

5. Add the zucchini noodles and cook for 5 minutes or until tender.

6. Serve warm.

8. Lentil and Vegetable Stew

Serves: 4 | Prep time: 15 minutes | Cook time: 25 minutes

Ingredients with GI value:

- Lentils (GI: 0)
- Carrots (GI: 16)
- Potatoes (GI: 77)
- Onion (GI: 10)
- Garlic (GI: 0)
- Tomatoes (GI: 15)
- Vegetable broth (GI: 0)

- Olive oil (GI: 0)

- Salt and pepper (GI: 0)

Directions:

1. Heat olive oil in a large pot over medium heat.

2. Add the onion, garlic, carrots, potatoes, and lentils and cook until softened.

3. Add the tomatoes, vegetable broth, salt, and pepper and bring to a simmer.

4. Reduce the heat to low and simmer for 25 minutes or until the lentils and vegetables are tender.

5. Serve warm.

9. Grilled Chicken and Vegetable Skewers

Serves: 4 | Prep time: 15 minutes | Cook time: 10 minutes

Ingredients with GI value:

- Chicken breasts (GI: 0)

- Bell peppers (GI: 0)

- Onions (GI: 10)

- Zucchini (GI: 0)

- Cherry tomatoes (GI: 15)

- Olive oil (GI: 0)

- Salt and pepper (GI: 0)

Directions:

1. Cut the chicken into cubes.

2. Cut the bell peppers, onions, and zucchini into cubes.

3. Preheat a grill or grill pan over medium heat.

4. Thread the chicken, bell peppers, onions, zucchini, and cherry tomatoes onto skewers.

5. Drizzle with olive oil and sprinkle with salt and pepper.

6. Grill for 10 minutes or until the chicken is cooked through.

7. Serve with a side salad or rice.

10. Baked Sweet Potato with Greek Yogurt and Honey

Serves: 4 | Prep time: 15 minutes | Cook time: 45 minutes

Ingredients with GI value:

- Sweet potatoes (GI: 44)

- Greek yogurt (GI: 0)

- Honey (GI: 0)

- Salt and pepper (GI: 0)

Directions:

1. Preheat oven to 400°F.

2. Place the sweet potatoes on a baking sheet lined with parchment paper.

3. Bake for 45 minutes or until the potatoes are tender.

4. Split the potatoes and top with Greek yogurt, honey, salt, and pepper.

5. Serve warm.

Snacks

1. Avocado Toast

Serves: 2 | Prep Time: 10 minutes

Ingredients:

- 2 slices of whole wheat bread (Low GI - 55)
- 1 ripe avocado (Low GI - 15)
- Salt and pepper, to taste

Directions:

1. Toast the bread in a toaster or in a skillet over medium heat.

2. Once the bread is toasted, spread the avocado over the slices.

3. Sprinkle salt and pepper to taste.

2. Greek Yogurt with Berries

Serves: 1 | Prep Time: 5 minutes

Ingredients:

- 1 cup Greek yogurt (Low GI - 24)
- 1/2 cup mixed berries (Low GI - 15)

Directions:

1. Place the yogurt in a bowl.

2. Top with the mixed berries.

3. Almond Butter on Celery

Serves: 1 | Prep Time: 5 minutes

Ingredients:

- 2 stalks of celery (Low GI - 15)
- 1 tablespoon almond butter (Low GI - 14)

Directions:

1. Slice the celery into thin sticks.

2. Spread the almond butter onto the celery sticks.

4. Apple and Peanut Butter

Serves: 1 | Prep Time: 5 minutes

Ingredients:

- 1 apple (Low GI - 36)
- 1 tablespoon peanut butter (Low GI - 14)

Directions:

1. Slice the apple into wedges.

2. Spread the peanut butter over the apple slices.

5. Cottage Cheese and Fruit

Serves: 1 | Prep Time: 5 minutes

Ingredients:

- 1/2 cup cottage cheese (Low GI - 13)
- 1/2 cup mixed fruit (Low GI - 15)

Directions:

1. Place the cottage cheese in a bowl.

2. Top with the mixed fruit.

6. Hard-Boiled Eggs

Serves: 1 | Prep Time: 5 minutes | Cook Time: 10 minutes

Ingredients:

- 2 large eggs (Low GI - 0)

Directions:

1. Place the eggs in a pot and fill with enough water to cover them.

2. Bring the water to a boil and then reduce the heat to a simmer.

3. Simmer for 10 minutes, then remove from the heat and let cool.

4. Peel and enjoy.

7. Kale Chips

Serves: 1 | Prep Time: 10 minutes | Cook Time: 10 minutes

Ingredients:

- 1 bunch of kale (Low GI - 0)
- 2 tablespoons olive oil (Low GI - 0)
- Salt and pepper, to taste

Directions:

1. Preheat the oven to 350°F.

2. Wash the kale and dry with a paper towel or kitchen towel.

3. Remove the thick stems and tear the leaves into chip-sized pieces.

4. Place the kale on a baking sheet and drizzle with the olive oil.

5. Sprinkle with salt and pepper and toss to coat.

6. Bake for 10 minutes, or until the kale chips are crispy.

7. Enjoy.

8. Edamame

Serves: 1 | Prep Time: 5 minutes | Cook Time: 5 minutes

Ingredients:

- 1 cup edamame (Low GI - 15)
- Salt, to taste

Directions:

1. Bring a pot of water to a boil.

2. Add the edamame to the boiling water and cook for 5 minutes.

3. Drain and season with salt, to taste.

9. Hummus and Vegetables

Serves: 1 | Prep Time: 10 minutes

Ingredients:

- 1/4 cup hummus (Low GI - 15)
- 1 cup chopped vegetables (Low GI - 15)

Directions:

1. Place the hummus in a bowl.

2. Top with the chopped vegetables.

10. Trail Mix

Serves: 1 | Prep Time: 10 minutes

Ingredients:

- 1/4 cup nuts (Low GI - 15)
- 1/4 cup dried fruit (Low GI - 15)
- 1/4 cup seeds (Low GI - 15)

Directions:

1. Combine the nuts, dried fruit, and seeds in a bowl.

2. Mix together until combined.

3. Enjoy.

Smoothies

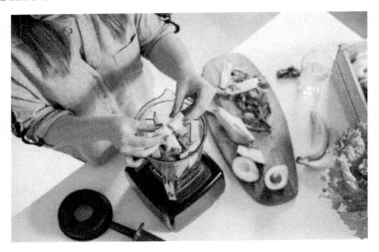

1. Banana and Avocado Smoothie

Serves: 2 | Prep time: 5 minutes

Ingredients (GI value):

- 1 banana (GI: 25)
- 1 avocado (GI: 15)
- 1 cup almond milk (GI: 14)
- 1 teaspoon honey (GI: 55)

Directions:

1. Place the banana, avocado, almond milk, and honey into a blender.

2. Blend until smooth.

3. Serve and enjoy!

2. Berry and Oats Smoothie

Serves: 2 | Prep time: 5 minutes

Ingredients (GI value):

- 1/2 cup oats (GI: 55)
- 1/2 cup blueberries (GI: 53)
- 1/2 cup strawberries (GI: 40)
- 1 banana (GI: 25)
- 1 cup almond milk (GI: 14)

Directions:

1. Place the oats, blueberries, strawberries, banana, and almond milk into a blender.

2. Blend until smooth.

3. Serve and enjoy!

3. Mango and Chia Smoothie

Serves: 2 | Prep time: 5 minutes

Ingredients (GI value):

- 1 mango (GI: 51)

- 1 banana (GI: 25)
- 2 tablespoons chia seeds (GI: 15)
- 1 cup almond milk (GI: 14)

Directions:

1. Place the mango, banana, chia seeds, and almond milk into a blender.

2. Blend until smooth.

3. Serve and enjoy!

4. Pineapple and Kale Smoothie

Serves: 2 | Prep time: 5 minutes

Ingredients (GI value):

- 1 cup pineapple (GI: 66)
- 1 banana (GI: 25)
- 1 cup kale (GI: 15)
- 1 cup almond milk (GI: 14)

Directions:

1. Place the pineapple, banana, kale, and almond milk into a blender.

2. Blend until smooth.

3. Serve and enjoy!

5. Apple and Spinach Smoothie

Serves: 2 | Prep time: 5 minutes

Ingredients (GI value):

- 1 apple (GI: 38)
- 1 banana (GI: 25)
- 1 cup spinach (GI: 15)
- 1 cup almond milk (GI: 14)

Directions:

1. Place the apple, banana, spinach, and almond milk into a blender.

2. Blend until smooth.

3. Serve and enjoy!

6. Carrot and Orange Smoothie

Serves: 2 | Prep time: 5 minutes

Ingredients (GI value):

- 1 carrot (GI: 35)
- 1 orange (GI: 40)
- 1 banana (GI: 25)
- 1 cup almond milk (GI: 14)

Directions:

1. Place the carrot, orange, banana, and almond milk into a blender.

2. Blend until smooth.

3. Serve and enjoy!

7. Coconut and Papaya Smoothie

Serves: 2 | Prep time: 5 minutes

Ingredients (GI value):

- 1 cup coconut milk (GI: 7)
- 1 papaya (GI: 60)
- 1 banana (GI: 25)
- 1 cup almond milk (GI: 14)

Directions:

1. Place the coconut milk, papaya, banana, and almond milk into a blender.

2. Blend until smooth.

3. Serve and enjoy!

8. Peanut Butter and Banana Smoothie

Serves: 2 | Prep time: 5 minutes

Ingredients (GI value):

- 2 tablespoons peanut butter (GI: 14)
- 1 banana (GI: 25)
- 1 cup almond milk (GI: 14)

Directions:

1. Place the peanut butter, banana, and almond milk into a blender.

2. Blend until smooth.

3. Serve and enjoy!

9. Beetroot and Almond Smoothie

Serves: 2 | Prep time: 5 minutes

Ingredients (GI value):

- 1/2 cup cooked beetroot (GI: 25)
- 1/2 cup almonds (GI: 14)
- 1 banana (GI: 25)
- 1 cup almond milk (GI: 14)

Directions:

1. Place the cooked beetroot, almonds, banana, and almond milk into a blender.

2. Blend until smooth.

3. Serve and enjoy!

10. Avocado and Flaxseed Smoothie

Serves: 2 | Prep time: 5 minutes

Ingredients (GI value):

- 1 avocado (GI: 15)
- 1 tablespoon flaxseed (GI: 15)
- 1 banana (GI: 25)
- 1 cup almond milk (GI: 14)

Directions:

1. Place the avocado, flaxseed, banana, and almond milk into a blender.

2. Blend until smooth.

3. Serve and enjoy!

CHAPTER 5

The 28 Day Low GI Diet Meal Plan

The 28-Day Low GI Diet Meal Plan is a comprehensive guide that outlines a scientifically-verified approach to diabetes control, weight loss and healthy eating. This meal plan is based on the Glycemic Index (GI) Food Guide Chart 2023, which was created to provide a scientifically-backed approach to healthy eating.

This guide provides a detailed list of low GI foods and recipes that can be used to create meals that are both healthy and delicious. The meals are divided into four categories:

breakfast, lunch, dinner, and snacks. Each meal includes a variety of nutrient-dense, low GI foods that are rich in vitamins and minerals. The guide also provides step-by-step instructions for creating a balanced and nutritious meal plan.

The 28-Day Low GI Diet Meal Plan is designed to help individuals achieve their diabetes control, weight loss, and healthy eating goals. This comprehensive guide provides a comprehensive overview of the GI index and explains how individuals can use it to create a meal plan that is tailored to their individual needs. Additionally, it provides in-depth information about each food group and offers tips and tricks for creating delicious and nutritious meals. By using this guide, individuals can take control of their health and create meals that are both satisfying and beneficial.

Week 1 Meal Plan: Day 1-7

Day 1

Breakfast: Overnight Oats (1)

Lunch: Tuna Salad (2)

Dinner: Quinoa Stuffed Peppers (2)

Snack: Almond Butter on Celery (3)

Smoothie: Mango and Chia Smoothie (3)

Day 2

Breakfast: Avocado Toast (2)

Lunch: Egg Salad (3)

Dinner: Creamy Butternut Squash Soup (4)

Snack: Apple and Peanut Butter (4)

Smoothie: Pineapple and Kale Smoothie (5)

Day 3

Breakfast: Egg Muffins (3)

Lunch: Avocado Toast (2)

Dinner: Cauliflower Fried Rice (5)

Snack: Cottage Cheese and Fruit (5)

Smoothie: Apple and Spinach Smoothie (6)

Day 4

Breakfast: Peanut Butter and Banana Toast (4)

Lunch: Greek Salad (5)

Dinner: Veggie Burgers (6)

Snack: Hard-Boiled Eggs (6)

Smoothie: Carrot and Orange Smoothie (7)

Day 5

Breakfast: Cottage Cheese with Berries (5)

Lunch: Salmon with Roasted Sweet Potatoes (6)

Dinner: Zucchini Noodles with Pesto (7)

Snack: Kale Chips (7)

Smoothie: Coconut and Papaya Smoothie (8)

Day 6

Breakfast: Omelet with Vegetables (6)

Lunch: Cauliflower Rice Bowl (7)

Dinner: Lentil and Vegetable Stew (8)

Snack: Edamame (8)

Smoothie: Peanut Butter and Banana Smoothie (9)

Day 7

Breakfast: Greek Yogurt with Nuts and Seeds (7)

Lunch: Cucumber and Tomato Salad (8)

Dinner: Grilled Chicken and Vegetable Skewers (9)

Snack: Hummus and Vegetables (9)

Smoothie: Beetroot and Almond Smoothie (10)

Week 2 Meal Plan: Day 8-14

Day 8

Breakfast: Steel-Cut Oatmeal with Fruit (8)

Lunch: Lentil Soup (9)

Dinner: Mediterranean Baked Salmon with Avocado and Tomatoes (1)

Snack: Avocado Toast (1)

Smoothie: Banana and Avocado Smoothie (1)

Day 9

Breakfast: Kale and Sweet Potato Frittata (9)

Lunch: Quinoa Burrito Bowl (10)

Dinner: Roasted Vegetable and Feta Cheese Salad (2)

Snack: Greek Yogurt with Berries (2)

Smoothie: Berry and Oats Smoothie (2)

Day 10

Breakfast: Whole-Grain Pancakes with Berries (10)

Lunch: Chicken and Roasted Vegetables (1)

Dinner: Baked Sweet Potato with Greek Yogurt and Honey (10)

Snack: Almond Butter on Celery (3)

Smoothie: Mango and Chia Smoothie (3)

Day 11

Breakfast: Avocado Toast (2)

Lunch: Egg Salad (3)

Dinner: Cauliflower Fried Rice (5)

Snack: Apple and Peanut Butter (4)

Smoothie: Pineapple and Kale Smoothie (5)

Day 12

Breakfast: Egg Muffins (3)

Lunch: Avocado Toast (2)

Dinner: Veggie Burgers (6)

Snack: Hard-Boiled Eggs (6)

Smoothie: Carrot and Orange Smoothie (7)

Day 13

Breakfast: Peanut Butter and Banana Toast (4)

Lunch: Greek Salad (5)

Dinner: Lentil and Vegetable Stew (8)

Snack: Cottage Cheese and Fruit (5)

Smoothie: Coconut and Papaya Smoothie (8)

Day 14

Breakfast: Cottage Cheese with Berries (5)

Lunch: Salmon with Roasted Sweet Potatoes (6)

Dinner: Grilled Chicken and Vegetable Skewers (9)

Snack: Kale Chips (7)

Smoothie: Peanut Butter and Banana Smoothie (9)

Week 3 Meal Plan: Day 15-21

Day 15

Breakfast: Omelet with Vegetables (6)

Lunch: Cauliflower Rice Bowl (7)

Dinner: Zucchini Noodles with Pesto (7)

Snack: Edamame (8)

Smoothie: Apple and Spinach Smoothie (6)

Day 16

Breakfast: Greek Yogurt with Nuts and Seeds (7)

Lunch: Lentil Soup (9)

Dinner: Roasted Vegetable and Feta Cheese Salad (2)

Snack: Hummus and Vegetables (9)

Smoothie: Beetroot and Almond Smoothie (10)

Day 17

Breakfast: Steel-Cut Oatmeal with Fruit (8)

Lunch: Quinoa Burrito Bowl (10)

Dinner: Baked Sweet Potato with Greek Yogurt and Honey (10)

Snack: Avocado Toast (1)

Smoothie: Banana and Avocado Smoothie (1)

Day 18

Breakfast: Kale and Sweet Potato Frittata (9)

Lunch: Chicken and Roasted Vegetables (1)

Dinner: Mediterranean Baked Salmon with Avocado and Tomatoes (1)

Snack: Greek Yogurt with Berries (2)

Smoothie: Berry and Oats Smoothie (2)

Day 19

Breakfast: Whole-Grain Pancakes with Berries (10)

Lunch: Egg Salad (3)

Dinner: Cauliflower Fried Rice (5)

Snack: Almond Butter on Celery (3)

Smoothie: Mango and Chia Smoothie (3)

Day 20

Breakfast: Avocado Toast (2)

Lunch: Avocado Toast (2)

Dinner: Veggie Burgers (6)

Snack: Apple and Peanut Butter (4)

Smoothie: Pineapple and Kale Smoothie (5)

Day 22

Breakfast: Egg Muffins (3)

Lunch: Greek Salad (5)

Dinner: Lentil and Vegetable Stew (8)

Snack: Hard-Boiled Eggs (6)

Smoothie: Carrot and Orange Smoothie (7)

Week 4 Meal Plan: Day 21-28

Day 22

Breakfast: Egg Muffins (3)

Lunch: Greek Salad (5)

Dinner: Lentil and Vegetable Stew (8)

Snack: Hard-Boiled Eggs (6)

Smoothie: Carrot and Orange Smoothie (7)

Day 22

Breakfast: Peanut Butter and Banana Toast (4)

Lunch: Salmon with Roasted Sweet Potatoes (6)

Dinner: Grilled Chicken and Vegetable Skewers (9)

Snack: Cottage Cheese and Fruit (5)

Smoothie: Coconut and Papaya Smoothie (8)

Day 23

Breakfast: Cottage Cheese with Berries (5)

Lunch: Cauliflower Rice Bowl (7)

Dinner: Zucchini Noodles with Pesto (7)

Snack: Kale Chips (7)

Smoothie: Peanut Butter and Banana Smoothie (9)

Day 24

Breakfast: Omelet with Vegetables (6)

Lunch: Lentil Soup (9)

Dinner: Roasted Vegetable and Feta Cheese Salad (2)

Snack: Edamame (8)

Smoothie: Apple and Spinach Smoothie (6)

Day 25

Breakfast: Greek Yogurt with Nuts and Seeds (7)

Lunch: Quinoa Burrito Bowl (10)

Dinner: Mediterranean Baked Salmon with Avocado and Tomatoes (1)

Snack: Hummus and Vegetables (9)

Smoothie: Beetroot and Almond Smoothie (10)

Day 26

Breakfast: Steel-Cut Oatmeal with Fruit (8)

Lunch: Chicken and Roasted Vegetables (1)

Dinner: Baked Sweet Potato with Greek Yogurt and Honey (10)

Snack: Avocado Toast (1)

Smoothie: Banana and Avocado Smoothie (1)

Day 27

Breakfast: Kale and Sweet Potato Frittata (9)

Lunch: Egg Salad (3)

Dinner: Cauliflower Fried Rice (5)

Snack: Greek Yogurt with Berries (2)

Smoothie: Berry and Oats Smoothie (2)

Day 28

Breakfast: Whole-Grain Pancakes with Berries (10)

Lunch: Avocado Toast (2)

Dinner: Veggie Burgers (6)

Snack: Almond Butter on Celery (3)

Smoothie: Mango and Chia Smoothie (3)

CONCLUSION

A Low GI diet is scientifically verified to be an effective approach for people with diabetes to control their blood sugar levels, avoid the onset of diabetes-related complications, and lead a healthier lifestyle.

This book provides a comprehensive guide to low GI recipes, including vegan, vegetarian, and gluten-free options, that can be incorporated into a 28-day meal plan for optimal health. Eating more fresh fruits and vegetables, whole grains, legumes, nuts and seeds, lean proteins, and healthy fats can help to lower one's Glycemic Index and reduce the risk of developing prediabetes. T

he Glycemic Index Food Guide Chart 2023 is an invaluable resource for anyone looking to improve their health and wellness by controlling their blood glucose levels and maintaining a healthy weight.

The Glycemic Index Food Guide Chart 2023 provides a comprehensive and scientifically verified guide to low GI recipes for diabetes control, weight loss, and healthy eating. The book includes a 28-day meal plan that is designed to provide a balanced diet that is low in GI and that helps to control blood glucose levels. The book provides an easy-to-follow guide to low GI recipes that are suitable for a variety of diets, including vegan, vegetarian, and gluten-free. The book also offers tips and advice on healthy eating habits, such as limiting sugar and processed foods and incorporating more fresh fruits and vegetables into your diet.

Ultimately, the Glycemic Index Food Guide Chart 2023 is an invaluable resource for anyone looking to improve their health and wellness by controlling their blood glucose levels and maintaining a healthy weight. The book is a comprehensive and straightforward guide to low GI recipes and meal plans that can help you achieve your health goals.

APPENDIX

Breakfast Recipes for The 28-day Meal Plan

1. Overnight Oats
2. Avocado Toast
3. Egg Muffins
4. Peanut Butter and Banana Toast
5. Cottage Cheese with Berries
6. Omelet with Vegetables
7. Greek Yogurt with Nuts and Seeds
8. Steel-Cut Oatmeal with Fruit
9. Kale and Sweet Potato Frittata
10. Whole-Grain Pancakes with Berries

Lunch Recipes for The 28-day Meal Plan

1. Chicken and Roasted Vegetables
2. Tuna Salad
3. Egg Salad
4. Avocado Toast
5. Greek Salad
6. Salmon with Roasted Sweet Potatoes
7. Cauliflower Rice Bowl
8. Cucumber and Tomato Salad
9. Lentil Soup
10. Quinoa Burrito Bowl

Dinner Recipes for The 28-day Meal Plan

1. Mediterranean Baked Salmon with Avocado and Tomatoes
2. Quinoa Stuffed Peppers
3. Roasted Vegetable and Feta Cheese Salad
4. Creamy Butternut Squash Soup
5. Cauliflower Fried Rice
6. Veggie Burgers
7. Zucchini Noodles with Pesto
8. Lentil and Vegetable Stew
9. Grilled Chicken and Vegetable Skewers
10. Baked Sweet Potato with Greek Yogurt and Honey

Snacks for The 28-day Meal Plan

1. Avocado Toast
2. Greek Yogurt with Berries
3. Almond Butter on Celery
4. Apple and Peanut Butter
5. Cottage Cheese and Fruit
6. Hard-Boiled Eggs
7. Kale Chips
8. Edamame
9. Hummus and Vegetables
10. Trail Mix

Smoothies for The 28-day Meal Plan

1. Banana and Avocado Smoothie
2. Berry and Oats Smoothie
3. Mango and Chia Smoothie
4. Pineapple and Kale Smoothie
5. Apple and Spinach Smoothie
6. Carrot and Orange Smoothie
7. Coconut and Papaya Smoothie
8. Peanut Butter and Banana Smoothie
9. Beetroot and Almond Smoothie
10. Avocado and Flaxseed Smoothie

MEASUREMENT CONVERSION CHART

Volume Equivalent (Liquid)		
US Standard	US Standard (Ounces)	Metric (Approx.)
2 tablespoons	1 fl.oz	30 mL
¼ cup	2 fl.oz	60 mL
½ cup	4 fl.oz	120 mL
1 cup	8 fl.oz	240 mL
1 ½ cup	12 fl.oz	355 mL
2 cups or 1 pint	16 fl.oz	475 mL
4 cups or 1 quart	32 fl.oz	1 L
I gallon	128 fl.oz	4 L

Volume Equivalent (Dry}	
US Standard	Metric (Approx.)
$^1/_8$ tablespoon	0.5 mL
¼ tablespoon	1 mL
½ tablespoon	2 mL
¾ tablespoon	4 mL
1 tablespoon	5 mL
1 tablespoon	15 mL

¼ cup	59 mL
½ cup	118 mL
¾ cup	177 mL
1 cup	235 mL
2 cups	475 mL
3 cups	700 mL
4 cups	1 L

Weight Equivalents	
US Standard	Metric (Approx.)
1 ounce	28g
2 ounce	57g
5 ounce	142g
10 ounce	284g
15 ounce	425g
16 ounce (1 pound)	455g
1.5 pounds	680g
2 pounds	907g

RESOURCES

Apps & Websites for Tracking Glycemic Index

1. Glycemic Index Tracker App (Android):
https://play.google.com/store/apps/details?id=com.go2glu.glycemictracker&hl=en

2. Glycemic Index Tracker App (iOS):

https://itunes.apple.com/gb/app/glycemic-index-tracker-gi/id1047883694?mt=8

3. Calorie Counter & Diet Tracker by MyFitnessPal (Android):
https://play.google.com/store/apps/details?id=com.myfitnesspal.android&hl=en

4. Calorie Counter & Diet Tracker by MyFitnessPal (iOS):
https://itunes.apple.com/us/app/calorie-counter-diet-tracker-by-myfitnesspal/id341232718?mt=8

5. WebMD Calorie Counter (Android): https://play.google.com/store/apps/details?id=com.webmd.android.caloriecounter&hl=en

6. WebMD Calorie Counter (iOS):

https://itunes.apple.com/us/app/webmd-calorie-counter/id411869885?mt=8

7. Glycemic Index & Load Calculator App (Android): https://play.google.com/store/apps/details?id=com.app.glycemicindexcalculator&hl=en

8. Glycemic Index & Load Calculator App (iOS):

https://itunes.apple.com/us/app/glycemic-index-load-calculator/id1089975739?mt=8

9. Lose It! App (Android): https://play.google.com/store/apps/details?id=com.fitnow.l oseit&hl=en

10. Lose It! App (iOS):

https://itunes.apple.com/us/app/lose-it-calorie-counter/id341232718?mt=8

11. MyNetDiary Diabetes (Android): https://play.google.com/store/apps/details?id=com.mynetdi ary.diabetes&hl=en

12. MyNetDiary Diabetes (iOS):

https://itunes.apple.com/us/app/mynetdiary-diabetes/id317914485?mt=8

13. Calorie Counter and Food Diary by MyNetDiary (Android):

https://play.google.com/store/apps/details?id=com.mynetdi ary.android&hl=en

14. Calorie Counter and Food Diary by MyNetDiary (iOS): https://itunes.apple.com/us/app/calorie-counter-food-diary-by-mynetdiary/id341232718?mt=8

15. Glucose Buddy Diabetes Tracker (Android): https://play.google.com/store/apps/details?id=com.azumio.android.glucosebuddy&hl=en

16. Glucose Buddy Diabetes Tracker (iOS):

https://itunes.apple.com/us/app/glucosebuddy-diabetes-tracker/id341232718?mt=8

17. Diabetes in Check (Android): https://play.google.com/store/apps/details?id=net.diabetescare.diabetescare&hl=en

18. Diabetes in Check (iOS):

https://itunes.apple.com/us/app/diabetes-in-check/id341232718?mt=8

19. Glycemic Index Food Chart (Website):

http://www.glycemicindex.com/foodSearch.php

20. Glycemic Index Calculator (Website):

https://www.calculator.net/glycemic-index-calculator.html

Printed in Great Britain
by Amazon